Uninvited

... A True Story

By

Marjorie Bosworth

I wish to truly thank F.J. Beerling, without her help and encouragement, there would not have been a book.

I would also like to thank my husband Ted for his love and patience and for fighting back when the lunatic attacked him. It saved our lives and without him by my side, I could not have gotten through this.

"We settled down to watch a film with the lights off, now we sleep with the lights on. The events that took place on that fateful night can only be described as a scene from a horror film, a nightmare…

…And for us, the nightmare continues."

- Marjorie Bosworth

Contents

Chapter 1
Texas Ted 1

Chapter 2
April 19th 21

Chapter 3
Uninvited Guest 29

Chapter 4
The Longest Night 44

Chapter 5
The Clean Up 56

Chapter 6
Arresting Evidence 67

Chapter 7
Guilty Or Not Guilty 81

Chapter 8
Hot Off The Press 99

Chapter 9
Life Goes On 105

CHAPTER 1

Texas Ted

Ted and I met quite by chance, although some people would call it fate. It was back in 1999 when I was living in Derbyshire, I would have been fifty-seven at the time and was fostering a young girl called Izzie. Izzie was twenty-seven and had been born with spina bifida and hydrocephalus.

Hydrocephalus causes a build-up of fluid in the brain and spina bifida is a birth defect that can lead to muscle paralysis, bowel and bladder control and spinal deformity. This meant that Izzie needed round the clock care. Yet, despite her challenges, Izzie was a bright girl and was curious to learn more about the world. She also loved to chat, so to help her to socialise and make new friends. My nephew, Gary, installed a programme on my computer. This meant that we could chat to anyone anywhere in the world, and that is when Ted came onto the scene or, rather, popped up on the screen!

I say 'us' because I would help Izzie with her spelling and sending emails and keep her safe when she was on the internet chatting with people.

Now Ted, who lived in Texas at the time, was just one of many people Izzie had chatted to and became friends with. It was all innocent. Izzie and Ted would chat for hours on end with me in the background keeping Izzie safe and I got to know Ted too, and as the months passed, we formed a close bond. Ted and I got on so well that one day, Ted decided he wanted to come and visit us here in England. Ted had never been to England before; Ted had never left America before.

Excited, we set a date and Ted came over to visit; that was in May of 1999. I went to meet Ted at Heathrow Airport in London, and when Ted got off the plane, I was there to meet him in person, finally, after months and months of chatting on the internet. I could feel my heart missing a beat; it was going to be a pleasure showing Ted around England. We had a wonderful time; I took him to many places, and he loved it. Ted flew over on a three-month visa and would stay with us until his visa ran out, which was in August.

Ted and I during a visit to Chatsworth House in England.

When it was time for Ted to go home, instead of saying our goodbyes, Ted asked me if I would like to go back with him for a holiday. I was thrilled and without hesitation, I said yes. I had never been to America before, and here I was about to go on a holiday for five weeks. I was so excited – it was an adventure to cross the pond. Izzie would be going to stay with my daughter, April, whilst I went on holiday in the USA.

When I got off the plane in Houston, I could not believe the humidity and heat that hit me in the face. "Get used to it," I said to myself, "You've got five weeks of this!" I was so excited.

Ted and I went to stay with Ted's mum. She had a house in the Rocky Mountains and the nearest town was one hundred miles away. Well, you can imagine how amazing the views were from her front porch; they were like nothing I had ever seen before and during the snowy season, you could stand on the front porch and pick out the mountain bears and mountain lions' paw prints in the snow!

I had the time of my life, and although Ted and I mostly stayed at his mum's house, we also went travelling across America and visited Ted's brothers and sisters – all five of them!

Ted had two brothers and three sisters; It was great meeting them; Ted had told me so much about them. First, we visited Lenny, Ted's younger brother, who lived

Ted and I at Key West's southernmost point.

In Key West, Florida. Wow, it was only ninety miles by boat to Cuba from Key West – I had never been so far away from my home in England, and I was living the dream of my life.

We visited Ted's younger sister Jane and her husband, who lived in Houston. Ted also had another sister Barbara, who also lived in Houston. Then we went on the ferry to Galveston; the ferry ride was free.

We continued our travels and went to visit Rebecca, Ted's other sister, in Austin, Texas. I was so excited to meet a real-life country and western singer, I love country and western music. Austin, Texas, is famed for its country and western singers, so Rebecca was in the right place at the right time to further her career.

Whilst we were there, Ted took me to a place called the Back Yard. It was really like a big park, and we went there to hear Willie Nelson sing. In America, people call their gardens yards. I had always played Willie's music back home and now I was going to hear him in person. Wow, life could not get any better.

Up to that point, I had led a sheltered life and going to America really opened my eyes, especially when, on another occasion, Ted and I were at an open-air country and western festival, and I saw young people taking drugs. I was horrified, but for them, it was part of their culture at that time. To me, it was my first time witnessing such a thing.

We stayed there for a week before travelling to visit Ted's younger brother Sam. Sam had an amazing career; he was a successful pilot and flew private jets for a Canadian Company. He had made his money and was living the high life – literally!

To hire the jet that Sam was the pilot and captain of cost around $75,000, which is around £60,000; in today's money, that's about £103,000.

We stayed with Sam for a few days and during that time, we went to visit the Texas School Book Depositary (now known as the Dallas County Administration Building). We stood at the window, which was allegedly the vantage point from which Lee Harvey Oswald shot President JF Kennedy. We had to climb six flights of stairs to get to it!

No trip to Texas would be complete without visiting the set of 'Dallas,' the smash hit American soap opera, famed for its feuding families, giant shoulder pads chandeliers and a lot of lip-glosses. But when we got there, it was not all lip-gloss and glamour; it was quite the opposite. The swimming pool was small, and so too was the set, but the rooms featured in the hit show were on show and although they looked much smaller than on the small screen, they were posh, plush, and perfectly presented.

The holiday was over, and we had travelled seven thousand miles in five weeks. Ted surprised me and asked me to marry him. We went to Mel Fisher's jewellery shop in the Florida Keys. He was the world's greatest treasure hunter, and there we bought two matching wedding rings made from gold off the Santa

Margarita. It was the Spanish Galleon that had sunk during the hurricane of September 6th, 1622, near Key West and we have the certificate of authentication to prove it. It was signed by Mel Fisher himself. Wow, I could believe that I was going to get married. We decided not to set a date at that time with Ted living in America and me living in England, but we had the rings, which, of course, I could not stop looking at.

Ted came back with me to England, and we made plans for our future together.

1999 was a happy and sad year; I had met Ted, but sadly my mum died in November. She was 95, I was devastated. Ted comforted me and helped me through the grief of losing my mum. He had to go back to Texas in January 2002 when his visa ran out. It was incredibly sad to have to say goodbye, but we had plans for me to fly back to America in March. Ted surprised me by saying, "Let's get married in Vegas,"

Back in England, I had lots to do to prepare for my wedding in Las Vegas; it was so exciting. I chose my dress with a matching jacket and some artificial flowers to go in my hair, with a matching bouquet, which I have to this day, sitting in a vase in my lounge.

My flight back to the USA was going to be my last! I was going to live in the good old USA, starting our new life together.

Ted met me at the airport in Houston, it had been a long flight and I hated flying, but I had something to look forward to. Ted drove me to Galveston, wined and dined me, showered me with flowers and chocolates, and we spent the night in a hotel in Galveston. Then we drove to Austin, where we were going to live after we got married. A couple of weeks before we got married, we travelled to Las Vegas and stayed in Vegas. Whilst in Vegas, we applied for our wedding license, which was a bit like going to the Registry Office in the UK.

Once we completed the form, we were given a date and could get married anytime, after the date. So, we chose the 28th of July in 2000. My goodness, how exciting and hot it was on the day of our wedding; it was 118 degrees!

We could have had a chauffeur driven air- conditioned stretched limousine to take us to the candle-lit chapel, but the hotel we were staying in was opposite the chapel, so we lost out on the limo ride. We spent our honeymoon travelling. We visited the Grand Canyon, which was spectacular, one of the world's seven wonders. We went to Indian Reservations, and lakes, driving into the mountains – Las Vegas is in the middle of the desert, so we travelled around it. We went to the Rocky Mountains and stayed with Ted's mum, now as her daughter-in- law.

Ted and I on our wedding day in a small candle-lit chapel.

Ted's mum was a lovely lady and a brilliant artist. We then drove to Austin in Texas, which was a long drive. Along the way, we stopped to take in the sights before reaching our destination, our new home! Ted had a job as a carpenter, and I had a new home to go with my new husband.

Whilst living in Austin, Ted bought me a little puppy, a tiny dachshund and we called her Molly. We stayed in Austin until November. Ted's mum phoned and asked if we could go and stay with her and help her to renovate her house. So, we went on our travels again, playing Willie Nelson's song, 'On the Road Again,' we always played that song when we went travelling. I was so excited, a new adventure for Ted and me and little Molly.

I had my first Thanksgiving dinner and Christmas dinner in America, whilst staying with Ted's mother, it was awesome.

We stayed with her for six months before travelling to Key West in Florida to do some work on Ted's brother's house.

We stayed there for a few months, and during that time, Ted bought us an RV (Motorhome), so I, Ted and Molly, the dachshund and Susie, the cat (Ted bought me a cat too) upped sticks and moved into the RV and then drove to Denver in Colorado in the Rocky Mountains. They call it the Mile High City because the elevation was 5280 feet from sea level – that was exceedingly high up in the mountains.

We parked the RV in the motorhome park in Denver in the Rocky Mountains. Living the dream every day. Everything happened at once, I got a new job as a social worker at the disability centre for independent living. I loved my job, I helped people to manage their day-to-day lives. It was extremely rewarding, helping others to get their lives in order gave me a sense of achievement and a sense of purpose. At around the same time, the owners of the motorhome park offered us to rent their cottage, which suited me, I was much happier with four walls around me. Eventually, we sold the RV.

Life was great for a long time until I went shopping one day and tripped and fell. I broke my femur, pelvis, and hip, but the bill for $100000 from the hospital and rehabilitation centre was even more painful. I had to spend three months in a wheelchair.

After my rehabilitation, Ted wanted to go back and live in Texas, which we did. We bought a house with five bedrooms, three en suite bathrooms and sixteen acres of land for the price same as my medical bills…!

The house came with one hundred Barbados sheep, two Pyrenees dogs, nine kittens, three dachshunds and a donkey called Elvis, and our pets came with us from Denver.

I had been advised to go back to England by the doctors after being diagnosed with osteoporosis and rheumatoid arthritis and could not get health insurance out in the USA, but we ignored this advice and stayed put.

Life in our dream home was short-lived, we had only been there for a year when I was diagnosed with cancer on my arm and without any medical insurance, we had to pay for all my treatment. Realising that it would run into thousands of dollars, we had to sell our five-bedroom dream house with sixteen acres of land, one hundred Barbados sheep, two Pyrenees dogs, nine kittens, three dachshunds and a donkey called Elvis, along with our own pets that came with us from Denver.

Not only did we have to sell up and find loving homes for all our pets, but it was heart-breaking. We also had to fly back to England and decided that we would bring our puppy Sunny back with us. Well, I had to fly back first because Sunny, our dog, had to spend six months in quarantine, so Ted stayed behind with him, plus I needed to start my cancer treatment and find us somewhere to live. Now, before I met Ted, I was born in England and from the age of fifteen, I worked and paid my National Insurance, so I was thankful and grateful to the NHS for the treatment I received.

I found a lovely three-bedroom bungalow in Glapwell in Derbyshire. It was owned by three sisters and had been their parent's home before they passed away. It was the sisters' inheritance, so I signed a contract with them for a year and six months later, Ted finally came to live with me in England in December 2008.

After the lease on the bungalow had expired, Ted and I moved to Tibshelf into another bungalow. It had a nice big garden and was surrounded by fields. We loved it there and in 2015, I went on holiday with my brothers and sisters. It was whilst on holiday that my older brother Andrew had become confused. It was the onset of dementia. When we came back off holiday,

I took Andrew to the Doctors and my worst fear was confirmed after a series of tests. Andrew knew something was not right, Andrew had lived in his bungalow in Sheffield for thirty years and I was thirty miles away in Derbyshire.

Worrying about Andrew, I would call him every day, nine o clock in the morning and six o clock at night. Although Andrew had carers, he deteriorated rapidly and would need twenty-four-hour care, not part-time care.

Andrew went into a care home, at around the same time that I was taken into hospital unexpectedly with a blood clot in my lung. During that time, Andrew grew very unhappy in the home, I guess he could not understand where I was. Andrew told Ted he did not want to stay there and that he wanted out, and that was when Ted said, "You can come and live with us," not really thinking this through. Our bungalow only had one bedroom and a small office, there was not any room for big brothers. Ted came to visit me in hospital and told me that Andrew was coming to live with us, "You're' kidding' was my response, "there isn't enough room."

I had almost died from an unprovoked blood clot on my lung and did not need the hassle at that time.

A couple of days later, I was discharged from the hospital along with a prescription for blood thinner for me to take twice a day for the rest of my life.

So, Ted went onto the internet and as if my magic, as if it were meant to be our dream bungalow, came up. It had land galore, four acres, it was detached, three good-sized bedrooms, a big bathroom, cloak room and even a separate toilet. It was like a mini version of the home that we had in America, only here in England.

So, a short while later, we signed the papers and moved in. We moved things around to accommodate Andrew, and a few months later, Andrew moved in.

During the time that Andrew lived with us, we made clever use of the land and bought five alpacas, three turkeys, ten ducks and twenty-four chickens. Ted was busy; he built barns and chicken runs and even put-up fencing. The alpacas were well looked after; people came from everywhere to see the alpacas and buy our free-range eggs. Andrew loved the alpacas', and we loved them too – although it was demanding work looking after the animals and looking after Andrew.

Things took a turn for the worse when Andrew decided to stop eating and drinking. At that point, we had no choice, but for him to go back into a care home, we did not spring chickens either, we were now in our senior years, and it was taking a toll on us too.

I went to visit Andrew every day until his last day. I sat with him, held his hand, and talked to him. I told him how I would take him past his bungalow on his final journey to his resting place, and I knew that he could hear me. A few days later, Andrew passed away peacefully.

Back at the bungalow, the animals still needed looking after, and people came for their eggs. Life was good after the sadness had passed. We were living in our retirement home, with nobody to bother us, just fields and trees, the kind of home anybody would want to live out their days in. Little did we know this would be lived; we s It was sad but necessary because now it was going to be our time for us.

The world was in turmoil, covid was everywhere and England was in its first lockdown on March 23rd in, 2020.

Ted and I said to each other, "Wow, aren't we lucky we are living in this paradise and don't have to worry about going out and getting infected." Everything we needed was delivered right to our door.

Little did we know that our paradise, our dream home, and life were about to turn into the worst nightmare imaginable.

"I never dreamt that going on the internet, helping Izzie to stay safe whilst she made friends and chatted from all over the world, that I would meet my future husband, I wasn't even looking for a relationship, I guess it was meant to be."

CHAPTER 2

April 19th

Sunday morning, 9 am.

S unday was our day of rest – there were no deliveries or post, so there was no need to go down the gravel drive, which leads to the gate we would open on weekdays to let in the postman and any delivery drivers. It was also a few weeks into lockdown, so nobody would be visiting either.

It was already a warm morning, by 9 am, according to the barometer stuck onto the office window, it was already 70 degrees, shorts weather!

We have a light breakfast on a Sunday because I would cook a roast dinner with all the trimmings and today, it was going to be roast beef and Yorkshire puddings. I had tea, and toast, and Ted had coffee and scrambled eggs. After breakfast, we would catch up on our emails and social media. This was now our only contact with the outside world since lockdown and formed part of our new daily routine. Asking friends and family how they were but did it remotely. It was a strange reality to be faced with.

Ted then decided that he would spend the day tending to one of the two-acre fields. Before, when we had the alpacas, they would chew away on the grass all day, keeping it short, but now they were gone, and the grass was getting long. There was a lot of grass to mow, so Ted bought a sit-on lawn mower, sat down on it, and set to work.

It took quite a few hours to mow the whole field, so Ted would mow it in shifts – some in the morning, some after lunch and then the rest by teatime.

I was in the kitchen preparing the Sunday lunch when I looked up and glanced out the window and to my surprise, I saw a man with two dogs wandering around up near the barns. The barns were quite a way from the bungalow, and we were in lockdown, so I was wondering what he was doing up there.

Curious, I grabbed the binoculars and took a closer look. Through the binoculars, I was even more surprised to see that he only had on a pair of shorts, no top, no socks, and no shoes. He then started to walk down the gravel path heading away from the barns and towards the bungalow. He was calling his dogs to make sure they followed him. He started to hobble because the pathway was stony, gravelly, and very uneven.

He carried on hobbling towards the bungalow; now, there was a fence between the bungalow and the upper fields. The fence was to keep the alpacas in and intruders out.

The fence also had a lot of signs telling people to keep out and that there was no public access, because it was private property. As the stranger made his descent,

I had now made my way into the field where Ted was busy mowing, and when the stranger was just a few feet away from the fence, he stopped and stared at both of us and did not say a word. I looked at Ted and Ted could see the stranger who then walked off towards the woods, and that was when we lost sight of him.

I turned to Ted and said, "That was a strange guy," Ted replied by saying, "Nothing strange about that, he is only walking his dogs, he is doing no harm," little did we know.

I took Ted's thoughts on board and thought no more of it, the stranger had gone and that was that.

This set of photographs gives you a visual perspective of the bungalow with the surrounding fields and countryside. Although what was to follow would change our lives forever before that night, the peace, tranquillity, and remoteness were nothing short of a never-ending dream.

This was the view of the barns in the distance from the kitchen window, where I was standing when I first caught sight of the stranger and his two dogs. This prompted me to take a closer look through my binoculars,

so, I wandered out into the garden (as in the photograph above), where I was able to get a better view of the stranger. When I looked through the binoculars, I was shocked to see that he only had on a pair of shorts, no top, no shoes, and no socks. I grew concerned.

In this photograph, you can see how remote the property was with nothing but the sweeping countryside and surrounding hills and woods. Being in lockdown, I wondered why the stranger was wandering around by the barns. Or even what he could be doing there.

In this photograph, the stranger would have been standing just beyond the fence to the left, and that was when he stopped and stared at us before wandering into the woods. He should not have been there; without exchanging cheery greetings with us, this was a cause of concern.

We carried on with our Sunday, it was now early afternoon and Ted had finished mowing part of the field and had come in for his lunch, our Sunday roast with all the trimmings. After lunch, Ted went back out to finish mowing the field. I sat out on the patio in my lounger, sunning myself, thinking how lucky I was to be living in this paradise, looking across the garden at fields and trees and perfect peace, no noise and nothing to disturb this tranquillity.

It was around 6 pm when Ted had finally finished mowing the field, all of it. He came inside and went for a shower. I had finished lounging in the sun a few hours before and had pottered around in the greenhouse tending to the peppers, cucumbers, and tomatoes – they were growing well in the massive greenhouse that Ted had built.

We sat at the kitchen table and had sandwiches for tea, strawberries, and cream for afters using the strawberries we had grown in the garden. Ted went for a shower, and I washed up and tidied around. When Ted finished, he came back in and we decided to snuggle up on the sofa and watch a film, which we did every Sunday evening. Snuggled between us was Cher, the long-haired dachshund who was fourteen and stone deaf, but we loved her.

Cher, sadly no longer with us.

"For the first time, I used my binoculars for purposes other than looking for deer, foxes and rabbits. Someone was acting oddly, and curiosity got the better of me. What was he doing out there and during a lockdown?"

CHAPTER 3

Uninvited guest

As we sat down to watch our film, I glanced toward the French windows to see a beautiful sunset. It was such a peaceful evening, almost perfect. I gave a sigh and thought to myself, "Life is good."

This photograph is just one of many amazing sunsets we get to experience from looking out across the fields from our bungalow.

About half an hour later, Ted suddenly turned the sound off on the television. I looked across at him and Ted said, "I thought I heard a ball bouncing." I said, "No, I did not hear anything," I replied. It was probably Tinker the cat, as he was outside. But Ted was concerned, so he got up and went outside and looked all around the bungalow but could not see anything amiss, so he cameback. We carried on watching the film then suddenly, we both heard a banging at the back door. It startled us both, all the gates were locked, and we wondered who could be coming to see us at nine-thirty on a Sunday evening.

Whoever it was at the door would have had to climb the gates or the fence to gain access into the garden. Ted got up and went to investigate, his approach was cautious, and I was not too far behind. We got the shock of our lives when Ted opened the back door and there, looming in the doorway, with a menacing look on his face, was a naked man. He must have been well over six feet tall because Ted is six feet one and the naked stranger towered over Ted. As soon as I clapped my eyes on him, I could sense that something was very wrong and that this was not going to end well.

The naked man then spoke to Ted as I was hovering in the kitchen and could see everything happening. What the naked man then said was genuinely bizarre, with his gaze fixed on Ted, he said, "I am (let's call him Mr X), and I am naked."

Ted said in a bewildered tone, "I can see that,"

At which point Mr X clocked that Ted had an American accent and added, "I am British, and I am moving in here, and you are moving out." There was a pause before Ted made the decision to shut and lock the back door. There was something very wrong with this situation. Mr X, on the other side of the locked door, reacted violently to having the door shut in the face and locked out; he started banging furiously on the back door. Ted had to think quickly, he did not know whether the naked stranger was going to harm us or just go away. Not wanting to take any chances, Ted remembered that he had a scythe in the garage with which he used to tackle the weeds. So, at the pace, he went into the garage and before he could come back into the hallway, Mr X was smashing the door down. He had put his fists through the glass panel at the top of the door, and then with an almighty kick, the door splintered just as Ted went past it before it crashed onto the floor, with shards of glass and splinters of wood scattering all over the floor.

I was still standing in the kitchen, unable to move. I was mesmerised by the unfolding events. Although Mr X was naked, he had managed to kick down a wooden back door with his bare feet. Capable of doing this, what else was he capable of doing, in what can only be described as a frenzied attack, on us, two helpless, almost defenceless pensioners in our seventies. Mr X was a lunatic, there was no other way to describe him.

I was still frozen to the spot and in the kitchen, memorised by what was happening, when Ted managed to shout across to me to dial 999 and get the police. I was in shock; we both were but managed to make our way out through the kitchen and headed towards the lounge. Just when we thought things could not get any worse, the naked lunatic ran around the garden and to the front of the bungalow. Ted made it in the lounge, saw the naked lunatic looking in through the French windows, and was muttering away. He then started to bang on the French windows and then started licking the glass!

He then suddenly grabbed an ornate iron BBQ that we had used as a feature and smashed his way in through the French windows. Although in fear of his life, Ted tried to reason with him, but it was clear that whatever was going on in this lunatic head, reasoning did not come into it. The lunatic had already made his plans.

Ted turned to me and shouted at me to get the police; I was in the hallway whilst all this was happening. It was as if a switch flipped in his head. The naked lunatic started screaming at Ted, "Take your clothes off and get on the floor, I am going to rape you and kill you!"

When I heard these words, I reacted badly and started to scream uncontrollably. Was I really hearing this? Yes, I was and that was when the naked lunatic grabbed hold of Ted's sweater and tried to pull it off, Ted fought back, he had to. This was turning into a life and death situation and Ted was not going to be raped by this naked lunatic, not today nor any day.

By now, I was trembling and still screaming uncontrollably as the naked lunatic started to beat Ted about the head with the broken BBQ, but something in me knew I had to get help, and through my screams, suddenly I came out of the stupor that I was in and although I was still shaking, I managed to pick up the telephone and dial 999. All the while, in my head, I was praying to God, "Please don't let this lunatic kill Ted."

How I managed to dial 999, I will never know, I was cowering in the corner and still screaming. I was in that room all alone and frightened to death. The noise coming from the lounge was almost deafening. It was constant, banging and shouting, this attack on Ted was blood-curdling, I could imagine what was going on in there, although I did not want to. It seemed like ages before the police answered my call, they asked me what the matter was and where did we live. I was still scream-ing and between the screams, I did manage to tell the police that a naked man had smashed his way into our home and was trying to rape and kill my husband. The police responded by asking if I knew the man! "No," I managed to reply through my screams, adding, "Can't you hear all that noise in the background?" The police then asked me if there was a place where I could lock the door to be safe. I remembered that we do not have locks on the doors inside our home, who does? The police kept telling me to take deep breaths and to calm down. How could I calm down? My husband was in the other room, beaten to death by a naked lunatic who had gone berserk. I wanted to help Ted and felt guilty that I was not in the lounge defending Ted. But calling the police was helping Ted, although, at the time, I did not realise it. I feared for my life as well as Ted's, and the feeling that I was going to die is a feeling I will never forget. It haunts me to this day. By now, I feared that Ted and I were not going to get out of this situation alive, it was an overwhelming feeling of desperation and despair.

In my mind, my thoughts were that if Mr X killed Ted, and then came after me, I would bleed to death. I was taking blood-thinning medication, it stopped the blood from clotting, and that thought turned into fear and kept me in a state of utter terror. All that time, the police kept saying to me, "You are not on your own, we are here." My response was, "I don't know where you are, but you are certainly not here." I did not mean to be curt, but they were not here. This was not their nightmare, they were not in fear of their lives, we were, and what was happening to us was very real indeed. My poor husband was fighting for his life and mine. Would the police make it in time? Were we going to get out of this alive? Under the strict instructions of the police, I stayed on the phone, Ted was still in the lounge when suddenly it went deathly quiet, there was no sound coming from the lounge, and at that very moment, I thought to myself, "Ted's been killed. Mr X has murdered my husband. My heart sunk, "That was it, I thought to myself, I'm next," Almost succumbing to the inevitable, although I did not want to die at the hands of this lunatic.

And I did not, for, at that very moment, I glanced across the room and through the window, I could see swarms of police officers running toward the garden and onto the patio.

I later learnt from Ted that towards the end of his attack, Ted had grown tired and stopped fighting back. He reconciled himself that he was going to die. How awful to get to the point when you can no longer fight for your life and resign yourself to the fact that you are going to die. Mr X was thirty-four years younger than

Ted, so Ted did well to put up a fight for as long as he did.

Whilst Ted was being attacked, I had been standing by the open window in the bedroom looking through it whilst on the phone to the police. I was still screaming and in shock and holding the phone up to my ear. The only sense of relief came from the voice down the end of the telephone telling me to take deep breaths and that help was on the way. After what seemed like an eternity, the police did finally arrive. They had jumped over the gate and were running towards the bungalow. I could not count how many they were, I was overcome with relief but frantically, concerned for Ted's welfare, I shouted to the officers, "My husband Ted, is he dead? Is he dead?" I then opened the bedroom door and went into the hall, which led straight into the lounge. The lounge door was open, but I did not go in. Frozen to the spot, nobody could have prepared me for what lay before my eyes. There was Ted, my husband of twenty years, slouched on the sofa with blood pouring from his head and all down his chest. His sweater was missing and all he had on were his jeans. Mr X was nowhere to be seen, but my thoughts now were for Ted and what he had been subjected to for him to be in that state. I ran into the lounge, not concerned for my own safety, but I had to get to Ted, I had to help him. I sat on the sofa next to him just as the policeman entered the lounge. The look on his face said it all, but he managed to compose himself and asked for the key to open the gate to let the ambulance through. Ted went into his jeans pocket, pulled out the key, and handed it to the policeman. The policeman handed it to another policeman through the broken French window door, who was standing out on the patio. - Everything was a blur, although I had managed to stop screaming, I was now shaking, and so too was Ted. We later learnt that this was due to shock, well it would be, after what we had just been subjected to, and whilst I may have been spared the physical attack, mentally I was broken, we both were.

Mr X had attacked the back door with his bare feet until it finally came off its hinges. Ted and I were petrified; we lived in the middle of nowhere, where there was nobody to save us.

In this photograph, you can see where Mr X had ripped the wood out and smashed the glass in the windows.

Another angle showing how much force was used to kick the door in and the damage it caused.

This photograph was taken from outside the French doors that lead out onto the patio. The sound of glass being smashed was ear-splitting and added to the terror.

This photograph of the ornate iron BBQ;i s as heavy as it looks. Not only was it used as a battering ram by Mr X to smash his way into our home, but he also beat Ted about the head with it. Ted is lucky to have escaped with his life.

To this day, I am still haunted by this image of Ted with blood pouring from his head down onto his chest. We are both in our seventies, and the shock alone could have killed either of us.

In this photograph, Ted was preparing to walk to the ambulance, despite having been beaten about the head.

In this photograph, you can clearly see the aftermath, the blood on the sofa, carpets and around the lounge. In the background, the broken French windows with glass all around.

"The feeling of disbelief and horror ran through my veins. How could this have happened to us? Innocent victims, living our lives, enjoying our retirement in beautiful surroundings. In a heartbeat, our lives had been changed forever."

CHAPTER 4

The Longest Night

The ambulances arrived, I guess they had been sent for when I telephoned the police. I never saw the naked lunatic after that, I guess they dealt with him on the patio. But the police asked for a blanket so they could cover him up. My look said it all, I was not about to feel any compassion for him after what he had just subjected us to.

I suddenly realised that our little dog, Cher was still on the sofa, she hadn't moved since settling down with us to watch the film! Cher was completely deaf. The paramedics worked on Ted, he was in a bad way and the lounge was full of paramedics and policemen, it was all quite overwhelming. Ted had lost a lot of blood, it was all over the room. His head was still pouring with blood, so they bandaged his head and his knee, which must have been batted by the BBQ as well. Ted's eyes had started to swell and turned back. It was not until sometime later that we found out Ted had a fractured cheekbone, ribs, and cuts and bruises. There were four big gashes on Ted's head, he had a terrible headache that lasted for days afterwards.

The police told Ted that they needed him to take off all his clothes and shoes – they were going to be used as evidence, and despite being a victim, their request made Ted feel more like a criminal. But understanding the need, he obliged, and I fetched him a clean set of clothes to change into. It would be over a year before Ted would get his clothes and shoes back.

I asked the paramedics which hospital they were taking Ted to. They said they would take him to Sheffield Hospital, over thirty miles away, but with extensive head injuries, Sheffield was the hospital to see Ted. One of the policemen was in plain clothes, came to me, knelt on the floor in front of me and asked me how I was coping. That was nice of him, he showed genuine concern and took the edge off what had just happened. I told him that I was fine, just traumatised and that all I wanted was for Ted to be taken to the hospital to have his wounds tended to. He was in so much pain, it was heart-breaking.

The police then told Ted that they were taking Mr X away, I guess they wanted him as far away from Ted and me as possible. Neither of us ever wanted to see him again. A few minutes later, a second ambulance came up the drive and was going to take Ted to the hospital. Yet despite having suffered horrific injuries, Ted managed to walk to the ambulance, assisted by the paramedics. Everybody walked through the smashed French windows, carefully stepping over the glass and debris scattered across the floor. It's now just me, Cher and two policemen in the lounge, in fact, in the bungalow, everybody was outside, and very soon, Ted would be driven by ambulance to the hospital.

The two policemen took me into the kitchen. The lounge was now a crime scene and had to be taped off. I would not be allowed to go back in there until the forensics had been in and carried out their investigations. In the kitchen, the policemen said its time to make a cup of tea, but to get to the milk, you had to go into the garage, where our big American fridge- freezer was. They had to cross through the crime scene, passing the back door, which was now on the floor, but they wanted a cup of tea and trod carefully, not disturbing anything. By now, I was starting to calm down and wanted my friend and neighbour, Angela, to sit with me, but the policemen said no because our home was now a crime scene. Well, I was not having any of this and I may have cried and seeing my distress, the policemen made a call and my friend

Angela was allowed to come and sit with me. In fact, she stayed the night, which was fading fast. I did not know this at the time, but Angela told me that after the attack, the lane was swarming with police cars, vans, and ordinary cars that had turned up to try and find out what was happening.

Angela and I and the two-policeman sat around the kitchen table, the police wanted me to make a statement, all I wanted to do was phone the hospital to see how Ted was doing, and besides, I could barely think straight. The police radios kept going off, the kettle kept going on and I was exhausted. I could barely process what was going on and was still very vague about what had just happened, trying to piece it all together in my mind was, at this stage, beyond me. It wasn't until the police explained to me that Mr X had two dogs, which they had to find as they had been reported missing, that point the penny dropped. As soon as they mentioned two dogs, I recalled the stranger that Ted and I had seen Mr X earlier that morning wearing nothing but shorts – he was the naked lunatic that had just attacked my husband.

The dogs were eventually found, they had been tied together under a bridge, not that far from the barns, where he was wandering around earlier that morning. The dogs were unharmed but very distressed and the mediator took them as, apparently, they were part of the crime scene!

Going back to earlier that morning, when I was looking through my binoculars at Mr X wandering around the barns; I had no way of knowing that he had been reported as a missing person along with his two dogs by his partner, who was six-months pregnant at the time. She had posted his disappearance on her local community page on Facebook. It also appeared on the missing dogs page in that area, everyone was concerned for the dog's safety and for his well-being, little did they know of the events that were unfolding later that day and not too far from where he lived.

Even before he had been wandering around at the barns, Mr X had knocked on the door of a cottage; it was the home of one of our friends, Daniel. The cottage was not too far from where he was wandering around, and he was fully dressed then. It was genuinely bizarre as he had asked Daniel for a dog lead, whilst standing there with his two dogs, who were not on leads. Daniel had replied to his strange request by saying, "I don't own a dog, so I wouldn't have a dog lead, would I?" and then added, "Are you going down to the farm," and with a vacant look in his eye, Mr X walked off without replying. The neighbour in the garden next door had heard the conversation, turned to Daniel, and said, "Wow, that was a bit odd."

When giving his statement to the police, Daniel told them that he thought there was something not quite right about him or his request, how right he has.

My friend Angela had now turned up to console me, but I think she also needed consoling when she saw the state of the place and the carnage that Mr X had caused.

It would cost us around five thousand pounds to get it put right, new doors, windows, sofa, and carpets which were covered in blood. As it was now a crime scene, Angela was escorted onto the property and into the bungalow through the front door. Once inside, we hugged, and I cried. I was so relieved to see my friend, given that Ted and I were facing a certain death only a brief time ago. I had so many emotions running through my body that it would take days for me to calm down, in fact, it took weeks. I even told the police that I could not stay in the bungalow. At the time, I just wanted to get away, as far away as possible. Everywhere I looked, there was blood, glass, and bits of wood. Our home had been violated and it didn't feel like home anymore. Our dream home, and our dream life had just turned into a nightmare, one which I would never fully recover from and never feel safe again.

With Angela to console me and the police making lots of cups of tea, the night soon turned into day, and I was still ringing the hospital every hour to check on Ted. Hours passed and without any notice, suddenly Ted walked in. The hospital had released him! Under any other circumstances, Ted would have stayed in the hospital, but as the attack happened during the lock-down, the hospital staff were frantic, all wearing masks and keen to tend to Ted and get him sent home as quickly as possible. Of course, Ted wanted to come home and so he did. We paid for the taxi and immediately, Ted wanted to go to bed. He complained that his jaw was hurting, Ted thought he had broken his jaw. X-rays were taken but were not looked at whilst Ted was in the hospital. Ted's head and knee were glued, and Ted was given leaflets on head injuries and what to look out for before sending him home. So, Ted went to bed, and his head started to bleed. The glue had come unstuck, as illustrated in the photograph below.

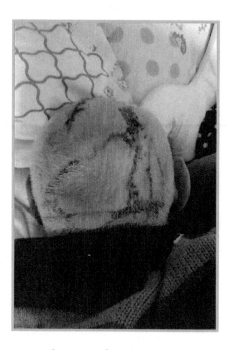

It was not the time for the two lovely policemen that had sat with me all through the night to go off shift. Their relief came in the shape of a police van. Inside the van was one policeman and one policewoman. Unlike their colleagues, they stayed in the van. I did offer them hot, but they kindly declined as they had bought their own. It felt a bit strange now, not being able to walk freely around the bungalow, I had to remember not to cross the tapes. I could not even go into the garage to get to the freezer, I would have to go a long way around, going outside to get into the garage.

That day was super busy, it was a warm day and after Ted came home, Angela also went home. It was just Ted and me inside the bungalow and the policeman and policewoman in the police van, just sat there, it was very surreal. I sat outside but had to keep coming back in because the phone kept ringing, it was constant. By now, word had gotten out, and friends were calling asking after us. In fact, strangers were calling asking how we were, I have no idea how they got our number, but it was nice of them to call.

What wasn't nice was the update on the local Facebook community page that Mr X and his two missing dogs had also been found safe. This was reflected in the comments box below, with people saying things like, "Oh, thank goodness you are safe and sound," and "So pleased that the dogs have been found too." Oh, the irony, Ted and I had been gagged (not literally) by the police stating that we were not allowed to comment. Not at least until after he had gone to court and was officially charged – this would take over a year, and during that time, we had to hold our tongues. Well, we are not holding our tongues now, this is the untold and uncensored first-hand version of events that took place on that fatefulday and the days that followed.

"Angry, we could not retaliate, we were not allowed to tell the world what Mr X had done to us, what he had subjected us to. We were reading messages of support – for him, not us. He had been found safe and well, which was far from the truth!"

CHAPTER 5

The Clean Up

The postman turned up, and curious, as you would be, he asked a lot of questions. "What's been going on here then," he quizzed, unprepared for what I was about to tell him. Well, the look on his face was priceless, and I then added, "Do you want to take a look?" to which he replied, "Go on then." So, making sure that the police in the van was looking in the opposite direction, which they were, I led the postman to the lounge door and opened it. "Wow, this is terrible, I have never seen so much blood and glass. It's like something off the television," he said, clearly shaken by what he was seeing. After that, he quickly went on his way, finished his rounds, and no doubt went for a cup of tea after seeing all that blood.

It wasn't long after that when a car pulled up and a man and woman got out. They introduced themselves as detectives from the local police station and were here to take a statement from Ted.

They sat down on some garden chairs with a table, so they could use it to lean against when taking notes.

I had to go and wake up Ted, I wasn't happy about this as Ted had not long been back from the hospital and was not only exhausted and mentally fatigued, but he also had a shocking headache and needed to rest.

Ted got up and went and sat out in the garden with the detectives. I was not allowed to sit with him then, so I put the kettle on and supplied hot drinks. My goodness, the interview seemed to go on for hours and I could see poor Ted struggling at times. It upset me, so I took myself off and sat on a bench near the kitchen window. I was too far away to hear what was being said, probably an excellent job as I was not ready to relive any of last night's events.

Whilst the interview was taking place, another car pulled up in the drive and a woman got out. She was also in an unmarked car and was here to take fingerprints and remove evidence from the crime scene, she was a Scene of Crime Officer (SOCO). She also came with a camera and spent a good deal of time taking photographs outside the bungalow, the doors, the glass, the broken BBQ, and anything related that would be used as evidence in court.

She was there for a good couple of hours and was very thorough. What with the policeman and policewoman sitting in the van, Ted and the detectives sitting at the end of the garden, and a SOCO taking a lot of photographs, it was like something you would watch on the television, but something was missing, all of Mr X's clothing. Even the shorts he was wearing earlier that morning had gone.

The police searched around the bungalow, all around the grounds and even up by the barns where he had been, but they could not find them. It was as if they had simply disappeared and to this day, they have never been found.

A man in a van turned up to board up the doors and windows until they could be repaired.

Before he had the chance to unlock the van doors, the police got to him and told him that he could not do anything until the SOCO had finished. It was quite busy, and all Ted and I wanted to do was go to bed, sleep, and forget all about it.

When the SOCO had finished and left and the windows and doors had been boarded up, everyone left, leaving Ted and me alone at last. But not quite, because at that moment, the postman and his wife had turned up. The postman had told his wife about what had happened to Ted and me, and they had come to look and see if they could assist with cleaning up and getting the blood stains out of the carpet and off the sofa. It was such a lovely gesture as, until that point, everything that had happened was procedure and protocol for want of a better word and now here, we were with offers of help to get our bungalow looking less like a crime scene and more like our home again.

A little later, I received a phone call, it was from one of the detectives that had interviewed Ted earlier in the day. It wasn't good news; it made my blood boil. I was expecting to hear that they had charged Mr X with all sorts of charges. Instead, I was told that he had not been charged as he had been sectioned under the mental health act and was locked up in a secure mental hospital for the next nine weeks.

I was angry that he had not been charged, I could not understand why, maybe he was insane to do what he had done to Ted and me, but later it would come out that the attack that he carried out on us, mostly Ted was in fact, premeditated.

Later that night, I had to go and lock the gate, Ted usually did this, but he had gone back to bed after his interview, so I made sure it was locked.

The next day was Tuesday, Ted was feeling the effects of all the events that had taken place and so he stayed in bed; his back was very poor, so a day in bed with plenty of rest was the order of the day.

I had also been severely affected by what happened, which was apparent when I woke up with a sore throat; I wondered if it was because of all the screaming and the stress that Ted and I had been subjected to. Either way, it wasn't just a sore throat; I felt out of salts and was still frightened to death;

I guess it would take some time to process it all and feel safe again, if I ever could.

It didn't help when a stranger appeared, he had walked up the driveway, so I went out to meet him and question what he was doing there. I was on high alert, and anybody was now a suspect of ill intent. I was not wrong, the stranger spoke to me. Well, the neve of it, he introduced himself as one of Mr X's friends. I was quite shocked; I had had enough of it all and the last thing I was expecting was a visit from one of his friends!

He had come to offer his support, or rather offer up a glowing reference regarding Mr X's character as a person and that all his friends had been shocked by what he had done. He went on to offer to do any jobs that he wanted to do around the property. It was a rather odd thing to offer, and as I listened, it became apparent that this chap was trying to convince us what a nice kind man Mr X was, or rather was he trying to convince himself and his friends. He added how much Mr X loved his dogs, and he could not believe that he had tied them up under the bridge and left them. He went on to say that Mr X's mother wanted to see us. I had heard enough and although I cannot recall what I said to him, I remember giving him short shrift and he left. I immediately telephoned the police station and told them what had just happened. The police wasted no time and went around to Mr X's friend's house, his mother's house and all his friends and family and warned them that under no circumstances were they to approach Ted or me.

Later that day, I received another visit, this time, it was a welcome visit from our postman and his wife and all their cleaning equipment. They had promised that they would come by after work and make a start on cleaning up the blood and the debris and would continue to do so every day after work until the bungalow once again looked like our home. Except for the broken glass, the doors were boarded up and would be boarded up for a month because the country was in lockdown and unable to have fitters come out to measure up and replace the glass. It was gloomy, but it wasn't forever.

After the postman and his wife went, it was getting late, so I went out and locked the gate. I was glad to go to bed and get some rest. Although I was still angry about the unwanted visitor, I knew I had to put it to the back of my mind and look forward.

The next morning, I was still very much the same, and was convinced that I had laryngitis. Every word that I uttered was more like a whisper. Ted had got worse during the night. His face was black and blue and very swollen. He also had a black eye and was barely able to open his mouth. Ted was convinced that his jaw was broken, but surely if it was where the hospital would have told him?

Ted was in a bad way and under those circumstances, the doctor decided that a home visit was necessary. I had already opened the gate, so I didn't have to worry about her gaining access. It was only about half an hour later when the doctor arrived. She did look quite a sight; she was wearing a face covering, as was I. She was also wearing a plastic apron and gloves. She looked like she was going into the operating theatre, I wonder what Ted thought when he saw her.

She was very thorough and spent quite a bit of time with Ted. She examined his face but didn't think that Ted had a broken jaw. She also examined Ted's ribs as he was experiencing a lot of pain and discomfort in that area. After she had finished examining Ted, she offered him some pain relief and advised Ted to get plenty of rest but to get back in touch if he got any worse. We were thankful to her for coming to see Ted during the lockdown, she had shown great concern for Ted's welfare.

Later that day, my friend Angela popped by with her husband, Mick. They kept their distance, two meters always. They came with a hoover that could suck up all the broken pieces of glass from the lounge, the hallway, and the patio area. It was brilliant, it hoovered it all up.

It was amazing, over the days that followed,

Ted and I were touched by the outpouring of support and kindness shown to us from our friends and people in the community, offering to help with the clean-up and   to check on our wellbeing and check in on us from time to time.

Later that evening, the postman and his wife turned up, as they did the day before and continued to work on the carpets and furniture with their equipment on the areas that had been heavily blood-stained.

The next morning, Ted was still very poorly, and I was still only able to whisper. The phone rang, it was a consultant from the hospital wanting to speak to Ted.

I took the phone to Ted, the consultant told Ted that he needed treatment on his face.

It transpired that Ted had a fractured cheek bone. Although the doctor who came out to visit Ted was thorough, perhaps something like a fractured cheek bone can only be determined by X-ray. And although quite unwell, Ted did not want to go into hospital. He had been through enough and did not want to be poked or prodded about. His head was sore and glued. His ribs were sore, his back was bad, and he just wanted to be left alone, so he was.

The community visits and goodwill gestures continued over the next few weeks and over the fence- people wore masks and offered up their gifts. We continued to be amazed by the outpouring from the people in our community, to this day, both Ted and I remain incredibly thankful to them for their support during the first few weeks after the attack.

"Poor Ted, with all the other injuries he had sustained, he was now recovering from a fractured cheek bone. Little did we know that this would haunt him for the rest of his life with that side of his face be- ing numb. A permanent reminder of what Mr X did to Ted."

CHAPTER 6

Arresting Evidence

A few weeks after the attack, Ted and I were recovering well from our physical injuries, but we were both beginning to show signs of mental fatigue and anxieties. We had never slept with the lights on before, but we did now, and the first was after the police had finished collecting evidence from the bungalow. That first night it was just Ted and me all alone at the bungalow in the middle of nowhere, surrounded by fields, terrified, and traumatised. It got to the point that Ted would walk around outside the bungalow and use his binoculars to scan the surrounding fields in case he saw something out of place and this was during the day! Night times were worse, we were reliving the events of that fateful night every night, and two years on, we still do.

We grew paranoid, being in our seventies and vulnerable, and now unsafe in our own home, we invested thousands of pounds on cameras and motion sensor detectors. Every angle of the bungalow could now be viewed from looking into the cameras and viewed on our giant television – all nine cameras and their viewpoint could now be seen by switching on the television. Our life was consumed by fear, and with cameras hooked up all over the place, we felt like prisoners in our own home.

We know from the police that Mr X was arrested and taken to the police station on the same night of the attack. We also knew he was not charged because he had been detained at a secure mental health unit.

It was nine weeks after the attack, and I had been ringing the police to find out if Mr X had been charged yet. Part of our fear was that he would be released free to roam the streets again. It was not good news, the police informed me that he had still not

been charged, but worse than that, he had been released and was now walking the streets a free man, whilst Ted and I were hiding away in our bungalow locked up like prisoners in fear of our lives that he would come back and finish what he started.

I was angry, furious, and very frightened. Even nine cameras and locked doors did not help me to feel less frightened. Was this feeling ever going to go away? What did we have to do to ensure that Mr X was charged and would go to prison?

I continued to call the police, applying pressure, but it never worked. I spoke to a few detectives, and although each one I spoke to say the same thing, they needed more evidence of Ted's injuries. I was getting desperate; in the end, I telephoned the hospital and after speaking to several different people, they provided me with Ted's X-rays and paperwork. I was doing well and called Andy, the detective who was assigned to the case; he advised us that there was not enough evidence to prosecute Mr X. At which point I grew desperate and wrote Andy an email. I needed to put into words how worried I was and to convey to him the sense of dread that Ted and I were feeling. I figured if I could get him to realise how much this was consuming our lives, he would do all he could to give us some peace and, of course, see to it that Mr X would be locked up for good.

This is the email that I sent to Andy on March 5th, 2021. I titled it 'An update on our feelings and fears that the man would walk free and go anywhere that he wants,'

"After many months of living in fear that the man would come back and attack us, we have never stopped watching. In case he came back, We dreaded the thought of dark nights and Morning. After the man was eventually charged and we were waiting to see if the case was going to court, it was a stressful time. He now knew he was going to be accountable for his crime against us. I think he thought he was going to walk away from what he did to us. Ted immediately increased our alarm system with 9 CT cameras playing and recording 24 hours a day, putting sirens at each end of the property with flashing lights. We have no neighbours, but hopefully, somebody will hear. The court date was set for 19th February, we were fearful that Mr X would come and take revenge on us now, he had been charged. I had counselling, but it had not helped so far, and Ted has awakened me from my nightmares. I am screaming and crying and having night sweats. We live in fear every day that he could be stalking us like he did that day. We would not know with all the fields and woods around us if he was. Ted continually rubs his face; he has never got back the feeling in it where Mr X fractured Ted's cheekbone.

This will be a memory of what the man did to him for the rest of his life. Our kitchen light has not been switched off since the 19th of April, the night of the attack. Ted and I are too afraid to be in complete darkness. Even in the daytime, when we are inside, our doors are locked, and our binoculars are always ready if we see a figure in the fields. We are too old for this; our lives will never be the same again. How can you ever forget seeing a 6ft 4ins naked man at your door, then smashing his way into your home and telling your husband he was going to rape him and then kill him. We feel like prisoners locking ourselves up, living in fear. But the man out there is free to do what he wants, who monitors him? We are told he has been warned not to approach us or our property. But who knows how his brain works? This does not make Ted and I feel any safer. Ted told me the other day that if he comes back here to get us, I am afraid I won't fight again. I feel too old and weary. We are now 69 and 77, completely innocent of any crime, locked like prisoners in our own home. We now wait for the next court hearing on the

19th of March. Please put him under lock and key and give us some peace. I don't wish him physical harm, but he should be accountable for his actions."

I also advised Andy that there were shreds of evidence, the hospital records, and the X-rays from Ted's injuries taken the night of the incident. This changed everything and after giving consent to the hospital to release the X-rays and reports to Andy, he visited us to take our statements and spent hours with Ted and me. He was shocked by what had happened to us and saw the extent of Ted's injuries for himself. This prompted Andy to act. He took the evidence back with him to the police station, along with our statements, and shortly after came the news that Ted and I had been hoping for, Mr X was formally charged, it had only taken a year since the attack!

According to the detective who formerly charged him with a section 20, wounding and criminal damage, when the charges were read out, the look on Mr X's face was priceless. He thought he had gotten away with it up until that point.

For Ted and me, it was a small relief. Our lives, living in our dream home, had turned into a nightmare, and despite receiving this news gave us little comfort. The twelve months leading up to his arrest were harrowing. We had taken steps to ensure we were as safe as we could be in our own home, but this new routine of sweeping the area, looking through binoculars, sleeping with the light on, and jumping when anybody came to the door was no way to live. I always had my mobile phone with me wherever I went, in case I needed to reach out and get help. Then the nightmares followed. I was sleeping, but even sleep didn't give me a break, I was even dreaming about that night, every night. It got too much for me, and in the end, I had to have counselling. Of course, still in lockdown, it was impossible to see a councillor, so my first lot of therapy took place over the telephone. If I am completely honest, it was a waste of time.

I had a second lot of therapy, but again I was not making any progress, this also took place with a therapist over the phone. It wasn't until the third lot of therapy that I could sit in the counselling room with the therapist that I began to make some progress. Ted, on the other hand, refused to have any therapy. I guess his way of dealing with it was to not deal with it. Not to talk about it, sometimes that is how people deal with trauma, maybe this was Ted's way of dealing with it too. Ted did not want to talk about it, I did, and I also wanted to put it behind us, we both did, and the therapy helped a little to achieve this. It also helped me to come to terms with what we had been through. My trauma counsellor suggested I write a letter to myself, over my feelings of guilt watching Ted being beaten whilst I was spared, and these are my thoughts written down in a letter,

"My husband was in the lounge being beaten by a 6ft-4ins naked guy fighting for his life. I was in a bedroom opposite the lounge screaming at the top of my head. I could hardly breathe of the feeling of fear he was going to kill us. But I managed to grab the phone and phone the police. I never know to this day how they could understand what I was saying with all the screaming and the shouting and banging from the lounge. They told me to lock myself in the bedroom and take deep breaths. We have no locks on our doors, but I closed the door. Don't put the phone down, we are on our way. You are not alone, they said, we are here for you. I remember saying I don't know where you are, but it's not here. I was praying to God not to let us die at the hands of this lunatic. The noise was horrific coming from the lounge. I tried to think about what I could do to help Ted. All I could think of was that we were going to die. But neither of us didn't, but Ted is left with mental and physical scars for the rest of his life, and I am left with the feeling of guilt cowering in the bedroom. What more could I have done to help him. I kept thinking, "After he kills Ted, he will come for me as soon as he hits me, I will bleed to death being on blood thinners." When I finally saw lots of police officers running across our property, I shouted, please help my husband, please to God that he's still alive. The police told me by phoning them, I probably saved our lives. That I should not feel guilty and did the best I could in the circumstances with that raving lunatic."

Although Mr X had been formerly charged, he was still free to walk the streets! That didn't help us at all, but at least we knew that the first step in bringing him justice had been taken and I was making a good recovery emotionally with the new counsellor.

Approximately one week after the attack, the victim support group got in contact and assigned us a victim support officer. Her name was Tara Ellis, and she was assigned to us on April 24th, 2020. Tara's role was to work with serious crime victims and advise us on how we could apply for financial help and counselling if we wanted it. I was already on my third lot of counselling, but at the time, I guess it gave us some comfort knowing that we could reach out to her if we needed to and to talk about what had happened. Tara was assigned to us for a year, we only communicated via the telephone because of lockdown, I never met her in person. I would also stay connected with the police on a regular basis, mostly to see if Mr X had been charged, but of course, he hadn't at that time.

After I was told that Mr X had been charged, I came off the phone, turned to Ted, and said, "He's been charged, finally. Wow, now we must wait for it to go to court, I wonder how long that will take."

The next visitor to the bungalow was Andy, the detective that had charged Mr X. He came to take statements from Ted and me that would be read out in court and form part of the evidence against him.

When Andy arrived at the bungalow, he spent considerable time with us, taking and advising of the court proceedings. Although at that time, we would not have to appear in court for the plea hearing. Giving our statements and reliving the events of that fateful night was harrowing, having to go through it all again was exhausting, too. Mentally fatigued, we ploughed on until both Ted and I had finished our statements.

After taking our statements, Andy then had to make an application to the magistrate's court for a hearing. It was up to the judge to decide whether the extent of the attack warranted the case to go to crown court.

Ted and I were nervous and very apprehensive. What if he was let off the charges and walked out as a free man. Would he want to exact his revenge on us for taking him to court, for exposing the truth of what he had done to us and what he put us through and still putting us through, reliving the nightmare every day of our lives? This left us feeling vulnerable and almost wondering if we were doing the right thing. However, it was the police that pressed charges, we didn't. Whilst he wanted revenge, I don't suppose it would matter to him who charged him, we were responsible for him being charged.

I was so fraught that I took to writing a letter to Andy. I wanted to share with him our fears and my feelings. I was worried that anything could happen between now and the hearing. At least if Andy knew how I was feeling, how worried and scared Ted and I were, he would do all he could within his power to act on our behalf to secure our safety and mental well-being.

We were assigned a witness support officer to prepare us for court. Her name was Jenny Gold, she was wonderful. Her role was to talk us through the court process, how it worked, what happened, and on hand to answer any questions we may have. Up until that point, we had never been to court, we had no idea of what to expect. Although Mr X had been charged, there was no injunction at that time. He could have if he wanted to take a wander across the fields and intimidate us. We had no idea what was going through his mind, but these thoughts of 'what if' were going through our minds and adding to our anxieties to the point that we stepped up our security and we're not sleeping properly.

Although it was only eight weeks until the court date, it felt like eight months. Ted and I were on edge the whole time, waiting, anticipating, and worrying.

When the court date for the hearing came through, Ted and I did not have to appear.

The hearing was to give Mr X the opportunity to plead guilty or not guilty.

During the weeks leading up to the hearing, Jenny Gold's support proved invaluable. Andy, the detective, was also in continuous contact with us, talking us through the process and updating us. We learnt a lot about the British justice system during that time. Still, we also wanted that time to come and go so that we could put it all behind us and continue our journey to recover physically and emotionally.

"Hoping that justice would prevail. Having enough evidence to support a case and for Mr X to be put behind bars for a long time, we were relying on Andy to build that case as Ted, and I tried to stay strong for the weeks ahead."

CHAPTER 7

Guilty or not Guilty

The day of the hearing finally arrived, and Ted and I were feeling all sorts of emotions and anxiously waiting for Andy to call and give us the verdict. I thought that Mr X would plead not guilty. All along, he had maintained that he could not remember a thing about that night, yet on that night, I clearly recall him saying to Ted, "My name is Mr X and I am naked."

We sat by the phone all day and finally, at around four pm, Alex called, Mr X had pleaded…guilty!

I was surprised, I really was, Mr X had maintained to the police that he could not remember anything about that night, why then would he plead guilty to something that he had no recollection of? But it didn't matter because by pleading guilty, he would go on trial at Derbyshire Crown Court and the date was set for Tuesday, June 8th, 2021, at 10:00. I would have my day in court and read out my statement of how I felt and what he had put Ted and me through and felt safe in the knowledge that Andy would be there to support me. Sadly, that was not meant to be, on June 7th, 2021, the day before Mr X was due to go on trial, I received an email from Andy, and this is what he said,

"Good evening, Marjorie. I was hoping to be able to attend court tomorrow and I had moved a few things around, but unfortunately, my Father-in-law passed away at the weekend and I need to be at home to support my wife and family.

On behalf of Derbyshire Constabulary and on a personal level, I would like to wish you all the best for tomorrow. The experience you and Ted went through was one of the worst incidents in my eighteen years serving in the police. Although I won't personally be there, I will be thinking about you during the day and will ring you on Wednesday morning to see how it went. Once again, good luck tomorrow," Kind regards,

Andy.

After reading Andy's email and learning that I would be going to court alone in the morning, I was devastated. Knowing that I had moral support from Andy and that he would be there in person to extend that support gave me the confidence I needed to stand up in front of the judge and read my statement. Now my confidence had hit the floor, I was nervous and anxious once more and unsure of the day ahead.

I didn't sleep at all that night. With so much uncertainty and the prospect of reading my statement out in court without Andy there to support me, I wondered how I got through the night, but I did.

I read my statement over and over; had I put enough words in, had I said enough, would it be enough to secure a conviction. Of course, these questions kept going around in my head and despite convincing myself that I could do this on my own, I was not sure I could.

I took one final glimpse of my statement before folding it up and tucking it safely away in my handbag, ready to read out in court.

In my own words, I wrote,

"Today, we would like to see justice and closure to the most horrific year of our lives, in which we have lived in constant fear.

We live in a bungalow in a 3-acre rural setting with no adjoining neighbours. We got the shock of our life on the night of Sunday 19th of April, when we heard loud banging on our door. My husband opened the door and was astounded and shocked to see a 6'4" naked man standing there. He said, "My name is Mr X, and I am na- ked." My Husband immediately locked the door. Mr X then battered the door down until it came off its hinges. He then ran to our patio and smashed the windows in, and he came into our lounge. He told my husband to take his clothes off and he was going to rape and kill him. You can- not imagine the terror and fright we felt. I could not stop screaming, "We are going to die at the hands of this man."

I screamed and screamed; I was hysterical. I grabbed the phone from our office, shut the door, and dialled 999. How I managed to do this, I will never know. My hands were shaking badly, my heart was racing so fast, and I honestly believed we were going to die. I thought there was nobody to save us from this lunatic. Until the day I die, I will never forget that evening. I close my eyes and it all comes rushing back as though it was yesterday, seeing my husband dripping in blood from his head and all the injuries he suffered at the hands of this man. He still is numb and has no feeling or sensation on the right side of his face caused by the fractured cheek- bone. We are old-age pensioners and liv- ing in fear. We now lock our doors day and night. We feel like prisoners in our own home. We moved here to have a peaceful retirement, yet we are now in a living nightmare & he has destroyed our lives. We are so afraid he will come back. Yet he gets to walk the streets while we live in fear. Most nights, my husband wakes me up as I now have nightmares and night sweats. I've had two lots of counselling, but it's not helped. I am con- stantly in fear and frightened. We have had to install an extensive alarm system with nine cameras around the property and two sirens at each end of the property. Our kitchen light is now on 24 hours a day. We are surrounded by woods and trees, which was what we wanted for the remaining years of our retirement.

Ted said to me the other day, "If he comes back, I'm afraid I won't fight again, I feel too old and weary." The guy was half my husband's age and in his early 30s. We are now 69 and 77, completely innocent of any crime, yet we have been made to feel like prisoners in our own home because of this man's atrocious actions. We are con- stantly on edge, watching in case we can see anybody. This man's actions have aged us, and have caused severe emotional trauma and permanent injuries to Ted.

Today, we hope for closure and to not live in fear anymore. We do not want this man to be allowed to walk the streets without a prison sentence. We want justice.

There was no going back, today was the day. We had waited for this day for almost a year, the worst year of our lives. We had been living in constant fear, we were on high alert, anxious and nervous all the time. Would there ever come a time when we could come down from this and these feelings? Hopefully, today will go some way to achieving this.

I was getting ready to go to court when the phone rang. The court clerk asked if I wanted to read my statement in court via a video link. Well, that was nice of them to give me the choice, but I was determined to have my day in court, face Mr X and read my statement in front of the judge. I declined their kind offer and told them I would appear in person. Still, in lockdown, the public gallery would be empty, where it was usually full of spectators, normally family and friends of the victims and the accused. Today, however, it remained closed to anybody.

As Mr X had already pleaded guilty at the hearing, there was no need for a jury to determine his innocence or guilt. It would be for the judge to hear the case for and against him, along with the evidence and my statement. Ted's statement was not going to be read out in court; Andy, the detective, was going to read Ted's statement out to the judge but being absent, it was never read.

I had never been to Derby before or Derby Crown Court, where I was now heading for the first time, and hopefully the last. I was not alone, my friend Jane called for me. She drove me in her car, that was nice of her, the journey took roughly an hour. Of course, at that time of the morning, the roads were already busy, Jane had to navigate through the early morning rush hour traffic and mums dropped their children off at school.

We finally found the Crown Court, it was a big imposing building. As soon as I saw it, I grew more nervous, I was hoping that today would be the only day and that justice would be served.

To the side of the Crown Court building was a carpark with a barrier. We could not drive in, the barrier was down, so we looked at each other and said, "Oh dear." At that moment, a man walked around the barrier from inside the carpark, and as he went past our car, Jane would like her window down and said, "Excuse me, can we park in there," to which the man replied, "I think that is reserved for the judges. Why, what business do you have here.? My reply was, " I am a victim and I have come to read my statement to the judge." The man said, "Please wait a moment," and walked back toward the barrier and made a call on his mobile phone. When he finished the call, he walked back towards us and said, "I am sorry, you cannot use this car park, but if you go back to the main road, turn right then left and right then, there is a public car park where you should be able to park." We thanked the man and off he went. We looked towards the court steps and about fifty people were now queuing to go inside. We were worried that we were late and would not be allowed to go in, so Jane followed the instructions given and we found a parking space, walked back toward the Crown Court and joined the queue.

The queue slowed and dwindled down. Everybody was standing two meters apart, wearing face-covering and being frisked by the security guards upon entering the court building.

When our turn came to be frisked, the security guards asked why we had come to court, so I told them that I was there to read my statement as a victim. They were fascinated and wanted me to tell them the outcome once it was over.

When I went through the metal detecting barrier, I had to leave my belongings and my walking stick. I was approached by two ladies who I had been told would be there to meet us, and escort you to where the trial was going to be held.

We went in a lift; I could manage all those stairs and Jane was happy that she didn't have too either.

Everybody was wearing face-coverings, it was very surreal, apart from the judges, they did not wear face-coverings.

We were taken into a side room and met our barrister; her name was Susie Brown, and She was going to be prosecuting Mr X. Also in the room were the two ladies who had escorted us into the side room and stayed with us. They offered us refreshments and made a very unpleasant experience less unpleasant. I could still feel myself trembling inside and was still very nervous, but not on my own, knowing that at any point, if I needed to go outside, my request would be accommodated.

Susie Brown talked to me, she put my mind at ease and said, hopefully, Mr X would be sentenced and sent to prison. "Hang on," I thought to myself, "What did she mean by hopefully? He had already pleaded guilty. Surely now, it was just a case of hearing the evidence and listening to my statement, which I was going to read out before sentencing was passed. Sarah had a copy of my statement and asked me if I had made any alterations, if I had, she needed to know so that she was in full receipt of the new information that I had.

But I had not added anything new to the statement. Susie also had a portfolio full of photographs that I had taken on the night of the attack. Most of them were of the injuries that Ted had sustained, and she was going to ask the judge if she could pass them over to him for examination and to be used as evidence against Mr X.

Susie escorted Jane and me out of the side room and back to the lifts. We went up to the next floor, along with the two ladies that had escorted us when we first entered the court building. It was full in the lift; thank goodness we were all wearing face- coverings.

We walked along the corridors, there was an eerie silence, apart from the sounds of heels on the floor. These corridors were usually full of the hustle and bustle, but not during the lockdown.

We sat down on a bench in one of the corridors. Susie had gone ahead and reappeared, escorted Jane and me into a small room, and closed the door. We were put in that room as Mr X was being escorted into the courtroom, and of course, we did not want to see him or be seen by him.

We were then taken from the small room and into court. Wow, it was huge, although the judge was not present at that time. I looked around the room and saw behind a very big glass petition Mr X with a warden standing next to him. I barely recognised him, I had only seen him that night (and earlier that day) without any clothes on. As I looked at him, he looked straight ahead, not at me.

I also saw a man, it turned out he was one of Mr X's relatives. At the time, he was looking down at the floor, I would say he looked very sad and sullen.

A few seats down from him was another man, who it transpired was from the press. The two ladies that had escorted us were waiting outside the door, they would be escorting us back out of the building once the case had finished.

Along with Susie, the barrister, Mr X's barrister was also there and about three of four ladies sat around, they were part of the court system and would be taking minutes from the events that would unfold during the trial.

After a few minutes, "All rise" was the vocal request from someone else in the room and that was when the judge entered, and I knew there was no going back.

When I clapped eyes on the judge, I did a double-take, I had seen that face before and turned to face Jane and said, "Oh my goodness, he was the man we spoke to outside the court when we needed a parking space. I thought his shirt looked expensive!"

The case got underway, and Susie wasted no time in putting our case forward. She was brilliant, the way she read out and presented the evidence was, in my opinion, enough to secure a conviction.

When she presented the judge with all the photograph evidence, most of the injuries that Ted had sustained, it was clear to see from the look on the judge's face that he was shocked. Even though he tried not to show it, I could see he was.

It was then the defence's turn to stand up and try to paint a picture of Mr X as a nice man who had set out that day to commit suicide and not commit what could have been a murder against an elderly couple.

He went on to say how Mr X's grandad passed away, and how his wife had left him and taken the children with her and now all these events had led Mr X to react so badly.

I sat there and felt sick to my stomach. Jane wrote a note and passed it to me as the defence was doing a good job championing Mr X's character. The note said, "He is going to get away with this." I nodded in agreement with her, it was possible that this was going to be the case and my heart sunk.

Susie then asked the judge if I could stand up and read my statement out in front of the judge and for all those present to hear. The judge's response to her request was, "Yes, of course, she can," so I stood up and, with hands shaking, I looked down at my prepared statement and in a clear voice and a deep breath, I began to read.

I had to stop a few times, it was very emotional, and I had to fight back the tears. My voice trembled, and my hands were still shaking, but I was resolute to fight back the tears and tell everybody in that room, especially the judge, how Mr X had not only half battered Ted to death but how he changed our lives completely and how we would never be the same again. I finished reading out my statement and stood staring at the judge. The room was still silent and then the judge began to speak, but I could not hear a word he was saying. I turned to Jane and whispered, " I cannot hear a word the judge is saying." So, Jane stood up and told the judge that I could not hear him. The judge asked one of the court clerks to provide me with a set of headphones so I could hear what the judge was saying. That was better. I could hear him now and I said thank you to him. The judge started to pull Mr X to pieces.

He turned to face him and said, "Everybody loses relatives, but they don't go out and do what you did to this couple. You went out with the alleged intention to commit suicide, but instead of committing suicide, you decided to attack this couple who did nothing to you. You ruined their lives, and they will never forget what you did to them. You say you cannot remember what you did to them, lucky you, you are spared that burden which they will carry with them for the rest of their lives.

He went on to say, "I am a judge, but I am also a person who would like to impose a longer sentence, but I am not allowed. The maximum sentence that I can give you today is five years reduced to twenty- either month because you have already entered a guilty plea."

He went on and added, " I am going to apply a restraining order of eight years banning you from going anywhere near this couple. You cannot go within a mile of them, their property, wherever they are, or whether they go. Even if they move, and this also applies to your family." After the judge finished speaking, Mr X's barrister stood up and made a verbal request stating that Mr X was full of remorse and can he write an apology letter? The judge quickly dismissed this request, reiterating that it was not allowed Mr X to contact us in any shape or form, including writing letters!

The judge then said, "Take him away," and that was it. Mr X was taken away, he was going to be locked up.

The judge stood up and then we all stood up. Then, the judge turned to Jane and me and said, " I am so pleased that you found a space to park your car in," and we all smiled at that. It took the edge off a very difficult day.

" I really believed in fate, and it was fate us meeting the judge and not even knowing that he was a judge, the same judge that would hear our case."

CHAPTER 8

Hot off the Press

The man from the press who had been in court taking notes wasted no time in getting the guilty verdict from into news by teatime that same day. Our story was splashed all over the internet – headlined in local and national newspapers, everybody now knew the full facts of what happened to Ted and me on that fateful day, and this is what they were saying,

Worksop Guardian

Thursday, 10th June 2021, 12:39 pm

Barlborough pensioner thought she was "going to die" during the home attack by six foot four naked 'maniac.' A 77-year-old woman told a court how she believed she was 'going to die' at the hands of a 'six foot four' man who appeared at her door completely naked and attacked her husband.

Marjorie Bosworth told Derby Crown Court to-day, "You cannot imagine the ter- ror we felt" as Mr X smashed his way through a window using a cast iron barbe- cue.

He then hit Mrs Bosworth's husband four times with the heavy garden equipment as her terrified part-ner tried to defend them both with a knife he had grabbed from his garage.

Prosecutor Susie Brown described how, on April 19 last year, at about 9:30 pm the elderly couple were watching television at their three-acre rural home in Barlborough when they heard a loud bang at the door.

Theodore Bosworth opened it and saw Mr X standing "completely naked", holding a bundle of clothes.

After Mr Bosworth, 68, managed to close the door, he ran to the couple's garage – finding a weapon to defend himself and his wife.

As Mrs Bosworth phoned the police, "Mr X kicked in the couple's door, threw the barbeque through a large window, and en- tered the property.

Circling Mr Bosworth with the barbecue in his hand, Mr X told him to "put the weapon down" and to "get on the floor and take off his clothes."

As the defendant tried to rip at his cloth- ing, Mr Bosworth "struck out" atMr X, at which point the defendant raised the bar- becue and hit him "three or four times" over the head.

For some unexplained reason, "Mr X ran out of the property! As Mrs Bosworth pleaded with the police to come.

When they arrived, they found Mr Bos- worth "covered in blood" with his trousers falling down and shirtless – while Mrs Bosworth was "inconsolable."

He spent three months in a hospital de- tained under the Mental Health Act fol- lowing the appalling incident.

Reading her victim's personal statement in court, Marjorie Bosworth described feel- ing like the couple were "going to die at the hands of this man."

She said, "Until the day I die, I will never forget that evening – I really believed we were going to die.

We are old-age pensioners living in fear and feel like prisoners in our own home – we moved here for a peaceful retirement, but we're now living a nightmare."

Mrs Bosworth described how the couple now had nine security cameras surround- ing their home and panic alarms on either end.

John Hardy, defending, told the court that Mr X had taken a cocktail of hallucino- genic drugs that night to end his own life following a mental breakdown.

This was brought about when the father- of-two lost access to his children and Suffered the sudden death of his father.

MR X of Barlborough, admitted a section 20 wounding and criminal damage.

Jailing him for 28 months, Judge Steven Smith QC said psychological reports painted Mr X as "Some- one who in normal circumstances presents as kind and warm."

However, he added, "You were far from that in April last year.

"Because of the state you were in, you re- sorted to taking substances – some of them hallucinogenic – such that you were re- sponsible for this dreadful affair.

"You destroyed the lives of Mr and Mrs Bosworth – who were in their retirement somewhere they had always wanted to be."

Judge Smith said instead of destroying his own life as planned, Mr X "Turned into the maniac in that field."

He added Mr X was fortunate to have "no recollection" of the psychotic episode "be- cause Mr and Mrs Bosworth do."

The same statement was also featured online in the…

Derbyshire Times (dailyadvent.com) In-YourArea.co.uk

" I was astonished to learn that even before I got home, the papers had got hold of the story and it had made the headlines in the national newspapers.!"

CHAPTER 9

Life Goes on

After I got back home, which was late in the afternoon, Ted greeted me, he was sitting out on the patio waiting for the news. After we had a hug, I told him that Mr X only got 28 months. Well, you could see the disappointment in Ted's face, even after I explained that the judge sentenced him to the maximum amount of prison he was allowed to award.

This was never going to be long enough; we were serving a life sentence, so why shouldn't he.

It was a feeling of relief knowing that he was now safely locked up behind bars, but for us, the adjustment of going to bed feeling safe would take a long time if we ever managed to feel safe again.

That first night, when we went to bed, I switched off the light for the first time in a year – this was a big step for us, albeit a small one in the great scheme of things, as we would have to learn to stop being afraid and work at getting our lives back on track.

One thing that did go through our minds was Mr X's family. How did they feel about Mr X being sent to prison? Would they want revenge? Was it possible that this was the beginning of a new threat from his family and even his friends? But we could not think like that. We tried, but it was a nagging thought that sat at the back of our minds, and as the days and weeks passed, I continued to have nightmares, which I have to this day.

One of the things that stay in my mind was when the Judge was passing sentencing and said to Mr X, "You are going to prison and when you come out of prison, you will still have your whole life in front of you, whereas this elderly couple won't have that privilege. You have taken away their rights to a peaceful retirement and instilled fear into them, which will never go."

What Mr X or the judge did not know about was the fact that Ted had been left with permanent numbness on the right side of his face, His cheekbone was fractured, which not only serves as a permanent re-minder that the feeling will never return, but the dam-age has been done. I watch

Ted often rubbing that side of his face, it saddens me deeply to know that he will never fully recover.

A few days after Mr X was sent to prison, Ted and I were contacted by the witness care unit. A lady called Angela Fenn from HM Prison and probation services, a victim liaison officer, was assigned to us and her role was to work with us, advising us and keeping us up to date on Mr X's movements. From what happened after he was released from prison, we would be told about anything he did. She was assigned to us for three years, and we still hear from her, she keeps us updated and for us, it does offer some relief. We definitely wanted to know where he would be living, but we are not allowed to know this information. We need to know what he is doing, it's part of our recovery.

Otherwise, we would be wondering and thinking up all sorts of things that would hamper our road back to recovery.

It was clear that the past twelve months had not only taken their toll on us mentally, but our physical health had declined. For me, I was not eating properly, I was experiencing headaches on a regular basis and it felt like there was constant pressure in my ears. It was so bad that I had a brain scan. I could not think straight and had stopped driving due to the headaches I was experiencing.

After several visits to my GP, she determined that it was a result of the physical trauma. Ted soldered on, the best he could, but he did contract a bad case of shingles. Again, my GP put this down to the trauma and stress he had gone through.

I was lucky enough not to get it, I had never had Chicken Pox, so I was spared!

The fear, the worry and the sleepless nights did not go away when Mr X went to prison. Any little noise would set Ted and

I off again, out came the binoculars and Ted did a sweep of the property. Anybody could come and, of course, living in the back of beyond, no neighbours to help. I suppose that part of it will never go away.

Sometimes, when I am out walking with Cocoa, I look around and appreciate the beauty, peace, and quiet. That is how I want to feel again, and Ted too. We desperately want to feel safe; we don't want intrusive thoughts taking over our twilight years.

It's impossible to ignore what has gone on, but it is possible to move on, hopefully, and look forward to the day when, for more than a few hours that, we can enjoy where we are, that a noise that we are unfamiliar with, no longer puts fear in our hearts.

Like Ted says, "Why should we let Mr X drive us away, control our thoughts when at some point he will be free again."

In fact, ten months after he was sent to prison, Angela, our Victim Liaison Officer, telephoned and advised us that Mr X would be released from prison. He had applied to be released and his application was accepted and in March 2022, he was released on license. Being released on license meant wearing an electronic tag and from 7 pm until 7 am, he had to be at home. Outside of those hours, he was free to roam the streets. This did little to aid our recovery and all the effort we had made to put this all behind us was hampered. It felt like we had gone backwards and then about a week after Mr X was released, he had an episode and was locked up in a mental hospital.

About ten weeks later, Angela telephoned me and informed me that Mr X had been released from the mental hospital. He was still tagged and living with a relative, so he was again free to roam the streets.

That was the last update from Angela. We know that this tag is due to be removed in August this year, 2022. His licence will continue until October 2023.

If Mr X does anything to break the conditions of his license, he will go back into prison. If he does not make such mistakes to break his license's conditions in October 2023, he will be a free man, untagged and free.

I would like to close by saying that Ted and I will never feel safe. We know that Mr X lives less than ten miles from us. Angela will only tell us if he does any-thing to break the conditions of his license, other than that, we could drive into town and see him.

Ted and I continue to make progress on both a physical and mental level. It is a long process and there are days when it feels like no progress is being made. We try to forget, but something will happen to trigger the trauma and relive the memory of what we were subjected to. If I'm honest, I cannot express enough the terror that still lives in our hearts. At our age, we should not be feeling or living like this.

Binoculars should be for enjoying the wildlife and identifying new species, not for identifying potential threats from fellow human beings.

This is us, Ted, and I, taken June 21st, 2022, after Ted received his British Citizenship. We continue to recover well, although I still suffer mentally from the trauma and ill-health. I am undergoing a series of tests to get to a diagnosis. Asides from that, I have a sunny outlook and remain positive. My favourite saying, "I am fine," has become my daily affirmation.

Printed in Great Britain
by Amazon

83049567R00071